Become an Explorer:
Make and Use a Compass

By Dana Meachen Rau

NORWOOD HOUSE PRESS

Norwood House Press
PO Box 316598
Chicago, Illinois 60631

For information regarding Norwood House Press, please visit our Web site at:

www.norwoodhousepress.com or call 866-565-2900.

Acknowledgements:
The author would like to thank George and Lyn Walker, co-presidents, Western Connecticut Orienteering Club.

Picture Credits:
cc-by-sa3.0*/Alvesgaspar/Wikimedia, 9; cc-by-sa3.0/Aney/Wikimedia (right), 25; cc-by-sa3.0/Greudin/Wikimedia, 37; Cepolina Photo, 39; Tamia Dowlatabadi, 16; cc-by-sa3.0/Typo/Wikimedia 8; cc-by-sa3.0/Iltsu/Wikimedia, 34; cc-by-sa3.0/Rémi Kaupp & Michael Daly/Wikimedia, 11; cc-by-sa2.5/Pavel Krok/Wikimedia, 25 (left); F. Lamiot/Public Domain, 33; cc-by-sa3.0/Leinad/Wikimedia, 36, 38 (right); cc-by-sa3.0/Patricio Lorent/Wikimedia, 10; Miaow Miaow/Public Domain (right), 41; Jeff Paris, 41 (left); Puco/Public Domain, 35; Dana Meachen Rau, cover, 17, 19-24, 26-30, 31 (right), 32, 42; cc-by-sa3.0/Una Smith/Wikimedia (left), 38; Ahmed Zahir, 7; Southmind, 12; Tom Stewart/CORBIS, 4; Kristian Stokholm, 43; Richard Styles, 5; Agata Urbaniak, 31 (left); Gonçalo Veiga/Public Domain, 18; Wildman, 14; Michal Zacharzewski, 40; Zenodot Verlagsgesellschaft mbH/Maler der Grabkammer des Menna/Public Domain, 6
*cc-by-sa= Creative Commons by Share Alike License

LIBRARY OF CONGRESS CATALOGING-IN-PUBLICATION DATA
Rau, Dana Meachen, 1971-
Become an explorer : make and use a compass / Dana Meachen Rau.
p. cm. -- (Adventure guides)
Includes bibliographical references and index.
Summary: "Includes the history of the development of navigational tools including the compass. Sections include a step-by-step project of making a functioning compass at home and then using the compass for orienteering activities. Glossary, additional resources and index"--Provided by publisher.
ISBN-13: 978-1-59953-383-4 (library edition : alk. paper)
ISBN-10: 1-59953-383-9 (library edition : alk. paper)
1. Compass--Juvenile literature. I. Title.
QC849.R38 2010
681'.753--dc22
2010010359

Manufactured in the United States of America in North Mankato, Minnesota.
158N—072010

Table of Contents

Learning to find your way in the woods using a compass and a map can add excitement to any family camping adventure.

Chapter 1

Easier to Explore:
The Compass Puts People on the Right Path

Camping in the woods can be an adventure. You can light a fire and toast marshmallows. You can sleep in a tent or even under the stars. You can also go exploring.

Do you want to investigate the source of the sound of running water? Are you curious about what lies over that hill? Where do those animal tracks in the mud lead?

A compass is a tool for exploring. Grab a compass and a map and let your curiosity lead you!

People have been using compasses for almost a thousand years. A compass holds a magnetic needle that points toward **magnetic north**. Explorers have been able to find their way around the globe using this small, handy tool.

A compass points to magnetic north.

Before the Compass

As long as people have lived on Earth, they have had to **navigate**. On land, travelers noticed landmarks, such as mountains, rivers, and trees. They used landmarks to navigate their way back home. They made maps using what they learned to show the next person the way to go.

But navigation was harder for sailors. The ocean looks the same in all directions. They needed to find a way to guide their ships.

They looked to the sky. Sailors knew that the position of stars changed depending on the ship's location and the time of year. They also noticed a point in the night sky that never moved from north—the North Star. In the daytime, sailors looked to another star—the sun. By measuring the distance between the **horizon** and the sun during the day, or the horizon and a star or constellation at night, sailors could figure out their north/south position, or latitude.

Sailors also relied on the wind. They could identify winds based on the direction they blew from and the type of weather they brought. If sailors wanted to travel south, they kept the cold north wind behind them.

But if the sky was cloudy, sailors could not see the stars or the sun.

Many ships did not even sail in winter. They waited for clear skies in spring to set out again. Sailors needed a tool to guide them in cloudy weather. They needed the compass.

Sailors used the position of the sun in relation to the horizon to navigate their way.

A Helpful Tool

Historians have traced the first compasses to ancient China before 1040 A.D. These compasses were made from lodestone. **Lodestone** draws iron objects to it and can also be used to magnetize iron. An ancient spoon compass was made of a lodestone spoon on a flat surface. The spoon spun until it faced south. The Chinese also made fish compasses. A very thin piece of iron in a fish shape floated in a bowl of water. Its head pointed south.

Europeans probably learned of the compass when traders visited China and brought the idea back with them. Early compasses in Europe were simply a piece of iron floating in a bowl of wa-

An ancient spoon compass from China was made of a lodestone spoon that spun on a metal surface.

ter. But sailors improved upon the design so it would be a useful tool for navigation. In the late 1200s and early 1300s, sailors started using a dry compass with a **pivoting** needle placed in a wooden box. They attached a compass card to the needle that showed the directions of the winds. This wind rose, also called a compass rose, helped sailors read their direction. It was called a "rose" because the direction points looked like the petals of a flower.

The compass greatly helped with navigation. Ships could travel year-round. More trade routes opened. Sailors used the compass to read ocean charts better. During the 15th and 16th centuries, explorers ventured into larger oceans. Christopher Columbus set out across the Atlantic Ocean. Vasco da Gama sailed around the southern tip of Africa. Ferdinand Magellan led the first trip around the entire globe. Even with compasses, though, explorers often went far off course.

The Wind Rose (or Compass Rose)

In medieval times, chart makers included a wind rose to show the direction certain winds blew. At first, the wind rose had 8 points, then 12. After the compass was introduced, it had 16, then 32. Today, compasses are divided into even smaller intervals, called degrees. A compass has 360 degrees.

This wind rose is from a chart dated 1492.

The statue of Flavio Gioia stands in Amalfi, Italy.

Flavio Gioia: Man or Myth?

In Amalfi, Italy, stands a statue of Flavio Gioia, the inventor of the compass. But most people do not think Flavio ever existed! Scholars do believe sailors of Amalfi may have helped improve the compass, but they do not believe it was the work of one person. They think many people contributed ideas to improve it.

A man named Flavio once wrote about compasses. Over time, historians think people may have misread documents mentioning Flavio the author and thought Flavio was the inventor.

The compass was not the only navigational tool on a ship. A chip log was made of a knotted line with a wooden weight that dragged in the water. Sailors dropped the weight overboard and let out the line. They counted how many knots they let out as the ship moved, and they kept track of the time. Since you calculate speed by dividing distance by time, they could determine how fast they were going. Speed on water is still measured in knots.

A chip log like this one was used for navigation on ships.

To measure time, sailors used an hourglass filled with sand. Soon they could better measure speed with the invention of the chronometer, a very accurate clock. Another tool, the sextant, better measured the distance between the sun or stars and the horizon to determine the ship's latitude. Sailors used these tools along with the compass to chart their paths.

More to Explore

Over the years, people tried to develop better dry compasses. But they found that compass needles would be drawn to the iron and steel of newer ships, and sailors could not get an accurate reading. The rough water of the ocean also made the compass card that showed directions spin wildly. In the 1800s, the

Liquid compasses are used on boats to give accurate directions.

liquid compass proved to be better for ocean travel. The compass bowl had a clear cover and was filled with a liquid that dampened the compass card so it would not swing as much.

Dead Reckoning

Longitudes are the lines on the globe that mark positions east and west. To figure out longitude, sailors relied on dead reckoning. Dead reckoning is keeping track of your position by knowing your speed over a certain period of time.

To calculate dead reckoning, sailors had to do some math. They multiplied the time it took to get from one position to another by the speed of the ship. But dead reckoning was not always accurate. Clocks could not keep accurate time. Winds and currents sent ships off course.

Many navigators still use dead reckoning today, but they have better tools than sailors of long ago.

The 20th century brought changes to the compass. **Orienteering** is a sport using a compass to read a map while hiking or exploring. Orienteering compasses were developed in Sweden as the sport evolved. On ships, the gyrocompass replaced many magnetic ones. This compass is not affected by **magnetic fields** or movements of a ship. It always points in the same direction. New methods of navigation replaced the compass, too. The Global Positioning System, or GPS, is used in many vehicles. GPS receives signals from **satellites** to pinpoint exact positions on the globe.

Thanks to explorers from history and to the technology of GPS, we have mapped most of Earth's surface. So what is left to explore? Plenty, and if you have a compass, you can do some exploring of your own!

Using a compass
and a map can
help you navigate
your way.

Chapter 2

Mighty Magnets:
How a Compass Works

Compasses seem to spin around in a funny way. So how could this little tool show you the way to go?

Why Does a Compass Work?

If you hold a magnet near something made of iron or steel (which contains iron), it will stick to the magnet. The area around a magnet is called its magnetic field. Think of it like a bubble around the magnet. When a nail is outside the bubble, it will not be drawn to the magnet. But as soon as it enters the bubble, the magnet pulls it close.

When two magnets get close to each other, they will either **attract** each other, or they will **resist** each other. This happens because all magnets have two **poles** where the pull is strongest. One end is called the north pole, and one end is called the south pole.

A magnet (like all things on Earth) is made up of **atoms**. Each of these atoms has its own magnetic field. In most objects these magnetic fields are pointing

True North and Magnetic North

When a compass points north, it is not pointing directly to the North Pole (or true north). It is pointing to magnetic north instead. This is because the "magnet" inside Earth is not perfectly lined up with the North and South poles. It is tilted slightly. This is called **declination**.

Declination measures the angle between true north and magnetic north in degrees. Declination is different depending on where you are on Earth. Magnetic north was in northern Canada in 2010. But this changes. Magnetic north is not in a fixed spot. Every day it wanders a bit. And over the years, it has shifted closer to true north.

in all directions. In a magnet, the magnetic fields are all pointing the same way. When you line up two magnets, the north pole of one magnet will stick to the south pole of the other magnet. The poles stick because the magnetic fields are pointing in the same direction. But if you line them up so that two of the same poles are together, the magnetic fields will not be pointing the same way. That is why they will not stick.

Earth acts like a giant magnet. This is called geomagnetism. (*Geo* means "earth"). Deep inside, Earth has a **core**

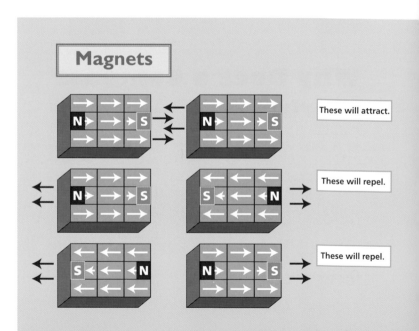

Magnets

These will attract.

These will repel.

These will repel.

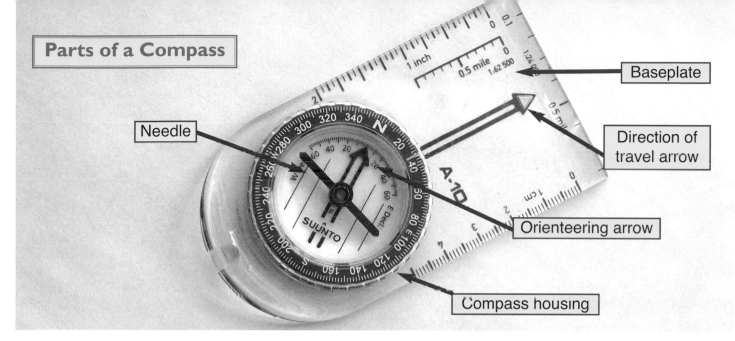

Parts of a Compass

Needle

Baseplate

Direction of travel arrow

Orienteering arrow

Compass housing

made of rock that is so hot, it is liquid. Earth also spins on an **axis**. Some scientists think that the liquid core and the spin of Earth create a magnetic field. This magnetic field is not very strong. But it is strong enough to affect other magnets on Earth.

That is why a compass works. The needle of a compass is magnetized. So when it is held in Earth's magnetic field (which means anywhere on Earth), the needle will point to magnetic north, just as two magnets attract each other.

Parts of a Compass

Let's look at the parts of an orienteering compass. The flat, clear rectangle of the compass is called a baseplate. The baseplate has an arrow called a "direction of travel," or DOT arrow. The compass housing sits on the other end of the baseplate. It is filled with liquid. The needle spins inside this compass housing. Half of the needle is red. This side of the needle will always point to magnetic north.

Around the edge of the round compass housing, you will see numbers. They divide the circle into 360 degrees. You will also see markings for the **cardinal points**. North corresponds to 0°, east to 90°, south to 180°, and west to 270°. These numbers help you read your **bearing**. Your bearing is measured in degrees.

The number dial on the compass housing turns. You will see another arrow at the bottom of the compass housing underneath the compass needle. You

Animal Compasses

Many animals travel thousands of miles over the same route each year. How do they do this? Scientists have found that some animals sense Earth's magnetic field. They have found magnetite in the bodies of bats, fish, birds, sea turtles, and other animals. These animals use their inner compasses to know where to go!

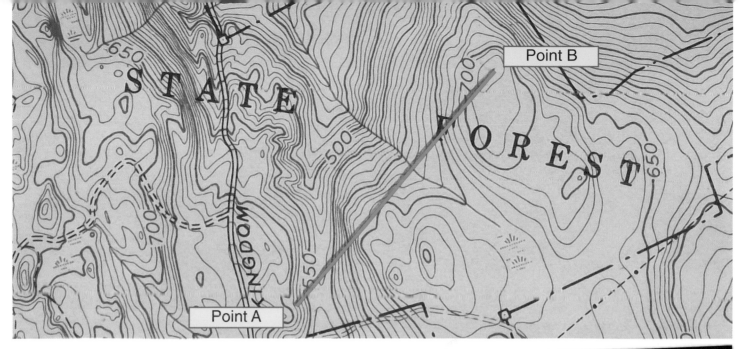

Point B

Point A

use this orienteering arrow to point toward magnetic north on a map.

Using a Compass and Map to Find Your Way

Try using an orienteering compass on a map. The job of a compass is to help you orient, or position, the map with the

You want to get from Point A to Point B.

land. First, figure out where you are on the map and then find the place where you want to go. Draw a straight line connecting the two points. On this map we want to go from Point A to Point B.

Next check the map for declination. Not all maps are the same, but some

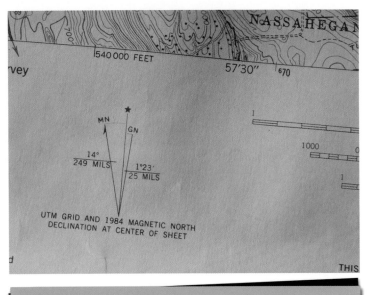

with true north. True north is always a straight line to the top of the map on U.S. Geological Survey **topographical maps**.

Since the declination on this map is 14°, you need to add 14° to your bear-

Line up the DOT arrow with the line you drew. Turn the compass housing to true north.

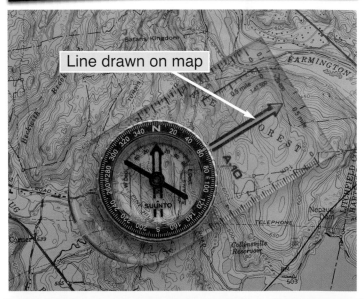

Line drawn on map

show you the difference between true north and magnetic north. On this map (above), magnetic north is 14° to the left of true north.

Now place your compass on the map. Line up the DOT arrow along the line you drew. Turn the compass housing to line up the orienteering arrow

ing. If magnetic north was to the right of true north, you would subtract. Turn the compass housing to the left to add 14°. Your orienteering arrow is now pointing to magnetic north on the map. Read your bearing by looking at where the DOT arrow crosses the numbers along the edge of the compass housing.

Now we can finally pay attention to the red needle! Take the compass off the map and hold it in front of you directly from your belly button with the DOT arrow pointing out. If you are wearing a belt with a metal buckle, do not put the compass too close to your waist. The buckle can affect the compass needle. Keeping the compass in position, turn your body so that the red end of the nee-

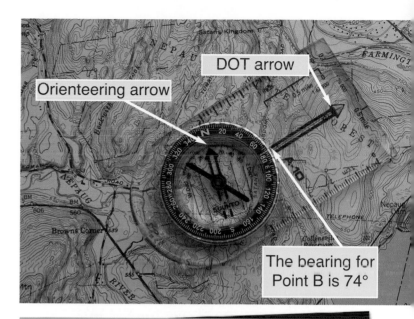

Orienteering arrow

DOT arrow

The bearing for Point B is 74°

The DOT arrow points where you want to go. The orienteering arrow points to magnetic north.

dle lies within the orienteering arrow. Some **orienteers** call this putting "red in the shed." The "red" is the needle, and the "shed" is the orienteering arrow." When you put "red in the shed," the needle is pointing to magnetic north.

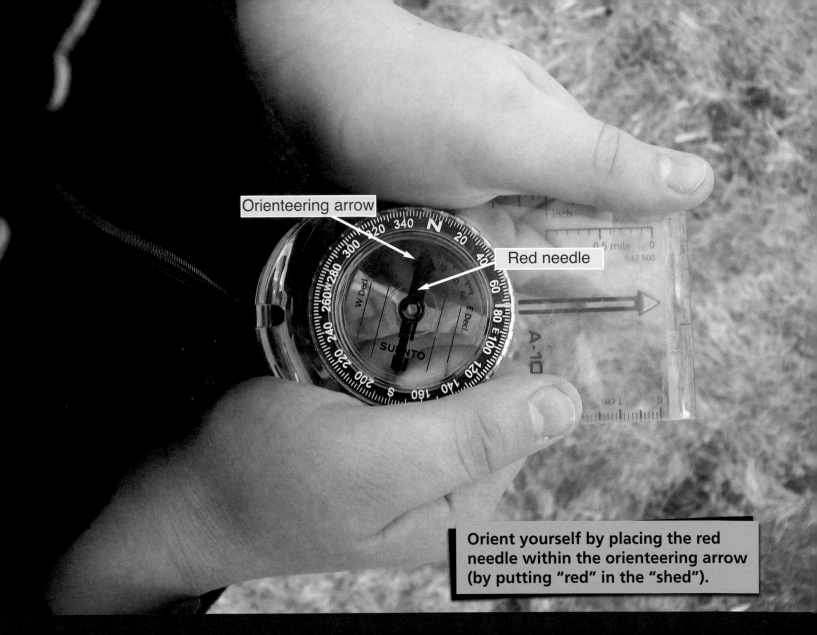

Orienteering arrow

Red needle

Orient yourself by placing the red needle within the orienteering arrow (by putting "red" in the "shed").

The DOT arrow is now pointing where you want to go. You have oriented yourself in the right direction.

You can try to walk in a straight line all the way to your destination, keeping an eye on the compass needle to be sure it stays within the orienteering arrow. But it is possible to stray off course.

It is better to pick something specific to walk toward. Find a tree that is along your direction of travel. Or have some friends run ahead and tell them to stop when they are still within sight and in line with your DOT arrow. Then walk to your friends, give them the compass, and you run ahead. It is like orienteering leapfrog!

You may not always be able to keep your bearing. Thick trees, a river, or a steep hill may get in your way. Look at your map. Perhaps you can take a different route around the obstacles. You may have to reorient yourself with the map to avoid them. Readjust your compass along the route if you need to.

Eventually, you will arrive at your destination.

Chapter 3

A Tool to Take Along:
Making and Using Your Own Compass

Which way is north? You can make your own compass to find out! You will be making a floating compass. The project will take you less than an hour. You might already have all of the items to make it right at home!

These are the materials you will need to make a compass:

 Round, clear, shallow plastic container and its lid Deli items, salsa, hummus, dried fruit, and other foods come in clear plastic containers. You can buy containers, too. A set of three containers and lids costs between $3.00 and $5.00.

 Steel sewing needle If you do not already have needles to use at home, you can buy them at pharmacies, superstores, or sewing shops. A set of needles can cost about $1.50.

✓ **Round lid from a milk jug** You can also use a nonmetal bottle cap or a round piece of cork. It has to be light enough to float on the surface of water. The milk will cost you about $3.50 or less a gallon. Just save the lid when you are done.

✓ **Bar magnet** If you do not have one at home, you can find magnet sets at many toy stores or craft stores. A magnet set can cost less than $10.00.

✓ **Water to fill the container** You can get this right from your kitchen or bathroom sink! If you want to use the compass outside, bring water out in a bottle.

✓ **Black marker**

✓ **One piece of white paper**

✓ **One piece of thick, sturdy 8½in x 11in (22cm x 28cm) cardboard**

✓ **Ruler**

✓ **Scissors**

✓ **Tape or glue**

needle

bar magnet

Step #1: Making the Compass Needle

The sewing needle is going to be the needle of your compass. But it is not magnetic on its own. You have to make it into a magnet by making all of the magnetic fields of its atoms point in the same direction. Right now they are pointing different ways.

That is where the bar magnet comes in. Hold the end of the needle with two fingers.

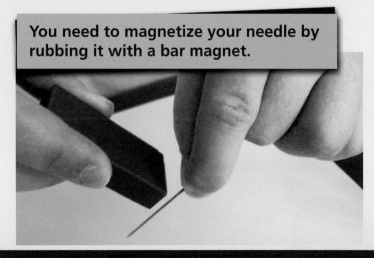

You need to magnetize your needle by rubbing it with a bar magnet.

How Refreshing!
Sailors would bring extra pieces of lodestone on ships to remagnetize the needles of their compasses. This was called "refreshing" the compass.

Your needle will lose its magnetic properties if you handle it too much. If it does, just stroke it with the magnet again.

With the other hand, hold the bar magnet. Stroke the north end of the bar magnet down the length of the needle about 20 to 30 times (or even more if you want) from the eye to the tip. Do not "scrub" the magnet back and forth on the needle. Start at the eye, stroke down, lift the magnet, and start at the eye again.

Test to see if your needle is magnetized. Place it near some paper clips. The paper clips should move closer to your new magnet! If they do not, try stroking the magnet again.

Step #2: The Compass Housing

The clear, round plastic container will be your compass housing. Fill the container almost to the top with water. Place it on a flat surface. Place the milk cap with the flat side down in the center of the water so it floats like a boat. Gently place your needle across the top of the milk cap.

Now watch what happens. Your milk cap might spin a bit. It might stray to the sides of the container. If it does, you can gently try to center the milk cap again. It will eventually settle in one place. One end of your sewing needle should be pointing north.

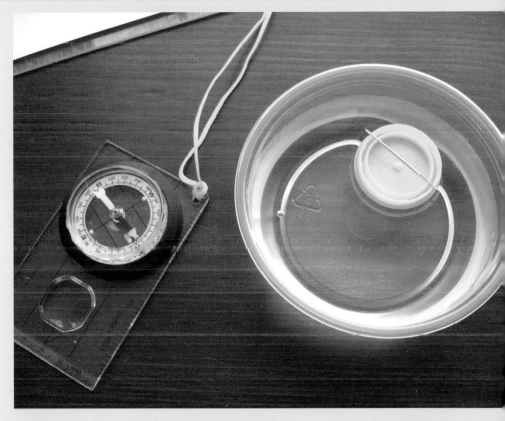

You can check to see if your needle is correct if you have another compass nearby. Make sure your bar magnet, paper clips, or anything metal is put away first, though. They can mess up your compass reading.

Step #3: The Compass Rose and Baseplate

1. Take the lid from the container and trace it onto a piece of white paper to make a circle. Cut out the circle with the scissors. Check to see if this circle fits flat on the top of your lid. If not, trim the circle until it does.

2. Now fold this circle in half and crease it. Fold it in half two more times and crease it well. Unfold. You should have four crossed lines.

3. With a ruler and black marker, trace over these lines so they are easier to see.

4. Then label the compass bearings on the lines going around the circle in the order below.

5. Along the line labeled N, make an arrow. This will be your orienteering arrow. Now glue or tape your new compass rose onto the top of the plastic lid.

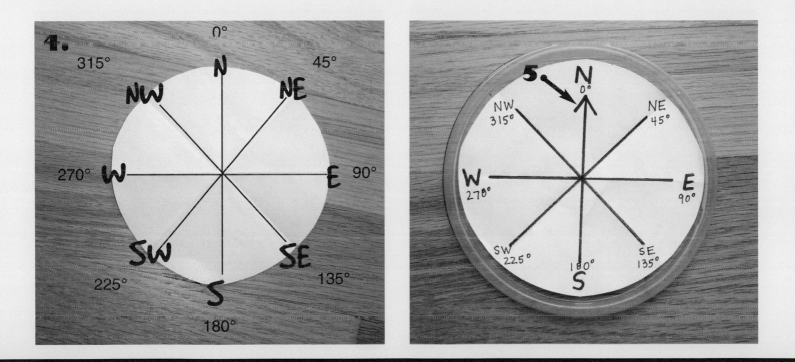

6. The cardboard will be your baseplate. Center the lid at the bottom of the card-board and trace a circle around it with the marker. This will be the spot where you will place your compass housing.

7. Draw a line from the center of the circle to the top end of the cardboard and place an arrow at the end. This will be your DOT arrow. Now you have a baseplate.

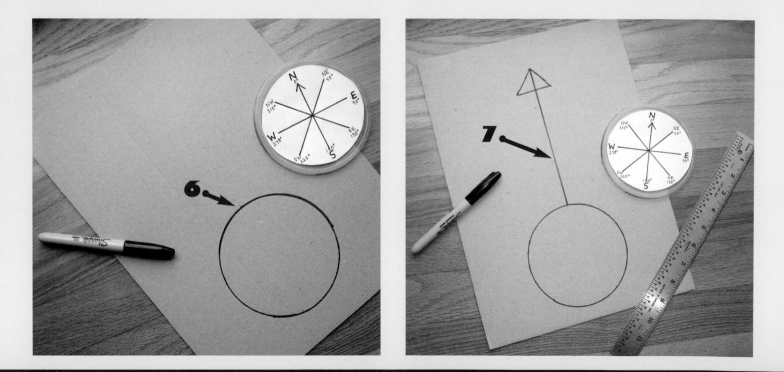

Step #4: Using Your Compass

1. Now assemble your compass, get your bearings, and locate a landmark. If you are outside, this landmark could be a rock, a tree, or even a friend (as long as he or she stays in one place). If you are inside, it could be a doorway, desk, or stuffed animal.

2. Place the cardboard (baseplate) so it lies flat on the ground or on a table. Put the lid onto the circle of the baseplate. It does not matter which way the compass rose is lined up yet.

1.

3. Place your compass housing (the container with water) on top of the lid. Now point the DOT arrow to the landmark.

You should be able to see the compass rose and orienteering arrow through the bottom of the clear container. Turn the lid (dial)

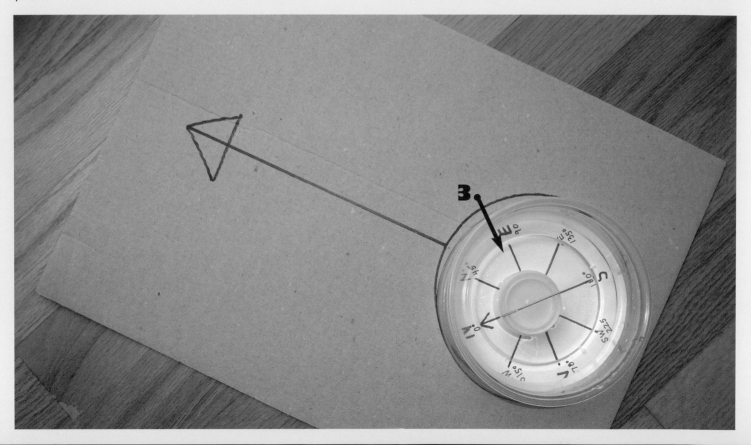

until your needle is lined up with your orienteering arrow. They may not be perfectly lined up since your cap floats around in the water, but they should both be pointing in the same direction.

Read the bearing of your landmark by seeing where the DOT arrow crosses your dial. Now you know the direction to go!

Which Way Is North?

If you do not have a compass, nature can tell you your direction, too.

Spot the sun! Hold up your watch so that the hour hand is pointing to the sun. South is halfway between the twelve and the hour hand.

See the stars! On a clear night, locate the Big Dipper constellation. Imagine an arrow running up through the two stars on the right of the "bowl" of the dipper. This arrow points ahead to a bright star: the North Star.

Look for **lichen**! Lichen does not grow well in bright sunlight. The north side of a tree gets less sun, so lichen grows on the north side.

Lichen grows on the north side of a tree.

Two men compete in a sprint orienteering World Cup race in Salo, Finland. Orienteering is a competitive sport.

Chapter 4

Setting Your Course:
The Sport of Orienteering

Orienteering is also called the "thinking sport" because it involves thoughtful planning and quick decisions. The object of orienteering is to use a compass and a map to find certain points along a course. People race to be the quickest to find the checkpoints and finish the course.

Types of Orienteering

Orienteering started in the early 1900s as part of military training in Scandinavia. People started to hold public competitions, and when the special orienteering compass was invented, the sport became popular.

Local orienteering clubs formed and organized events. Now people all over the globe compete in orienteering. Some people compete on cross-country skis or mountain bikes. Some orienteer at night with flashlights. There is even a World Orienteering

Winter orienteering competitions are conducted on skis.

An orienteering control point is set on a course in the middle of the woods.

checkpoints, called controls, marked at different places on a map. Once you have visited all of the controls in a certain order, you return to the finish line.

A score-orienteering course has many controls. Each control has a point value, and you can find them in any order. But there is a time limit. The controls farthest from the start are worth the most. The faster you are, the more points you get.

On a line-orienteering map, the controls are not marked. But the route is. By following the line, you discover the checkpoints. This tests an orienteer's use of the compass and ability to stay on course.

Orienteering courses are set up for all different skill levels and ages. Begin-

Championship, in which men and women race to be the fastest orienteers.

Point-to-point (or cross-country) orienteering is one of the most popular types. The goal is to visit a series of

ner courses might be only 1 mile (1.6km) or less with controls that are clearly placed and easy to find along trails. An expert course can be more than 10 miles (16km) with controls that are off the trails on more difficult to find land features, such as rocks, trees, or other areas.

Orienteering Tools: The Map, Compass, and Control Card

If you go to an orienteering competition at a forest or park, you'll be given a map. The map used for orienteering is a special topographical map. Orienteering maps have already been adjusted for magnetic declination. The top of an orienteering map is pointed toward

The Orienteering Map

Colors are important on a standard orienteering map.

- Black: roads, trails, buildings, and natural rock features
- Brown: contour lines to show the lay of the land
- Blue: water
- White: clear forest
- Green: thick plants that would be hard to hike through
- Yellow: a field or meadow

An orienteering map is an important tool to orienteers.

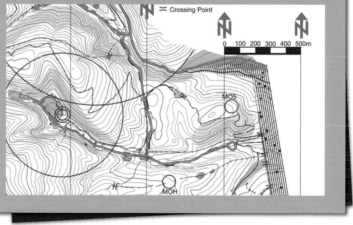

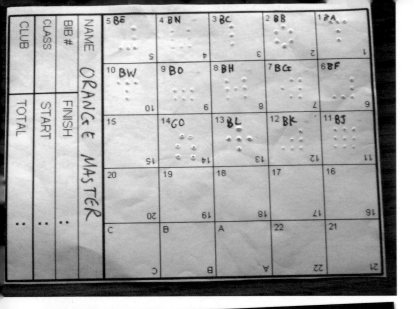

This orienteering control card is marked with 14 different needle punches from the control points on the orienteering course.

enteering course, a triangle marks the start. Controls are shown with numbered circles. The numbers tell you the order in which to find them. Sometimes the controls are connected by lines to show you the direction to go. A double circle marks the finish line.

You will also be given a control card. Controls will be at specific land features, like the crossing of two trails, a turn in a stream, or a big boulder. As you stop at each control, you punch your control card with a special puncher. Each

A thumb compass is the easiest to use while navigating a trail.

magnetic north and the vertical lines on the map can be used for setting your compass. The map has contour lines that show when the land gets higher or lower. Lines circling each other show a hill. Land is steep when you see lots of lines close together. On a standard ori-

control has a different puncher to prove that you made it to all the controls.

The most important tool is your orienteering compass. Some people use a thumb compass. This smaller compass straps to your thumb, so you can glance at it easily when you look at your map. You cannot set bearings on a thumb compass, though.

At each control, you place your compass on your map to set the direction to the next control. Then you use your compass to keep your bearings when you are on the move. Remember, it is a race. You need to be skillful using a map and compass and making

A man stops mid-course to check his position while sports orienteering.

choices. Which way will you go? How can you avoid the big hill? Will too many bushes block your way? You have to make fast decisions and hope they are the right ones.

Make Your Own Treasure Hunt

Step #1: Hide Your Treasure

First decide what your treasure will be. It could be candy, pennies, or directions to the next control. Then find four or five locations to hide your treasure around the yard, park, or room.

Next determine your starting point. From here, look ahead to where you will hide the first prize. Mark your bearing. Count how many steps it takes you to get there. Mark this down, too. Hide your treasure.

From your first control, look to the second point. Mark your bearing and hide the treasure again. Repeat until you have hidden all the prizes and reached the end.

You do not have to go to an organized event to practice your compass skills. Try setting up a treasure hunt in your own backyard, a nearby park, or your school yard. If you do not have an outdoor spot, you can do it in a classroom, too. Try using the compass you made yourself!

Step #2: Write the Directions

Now write out the directions. They might look something like this:

Start: Set your bearing at 225°. Walk 20 steps.

Control 1: Set your bearing at 90°. Walk 40 steps.

Control 2: Etc.

Writing your directions in a notebook before you start your adventure will help you keep track of where you want to go.

Geocaching Treasure Hunts

Geocaching is a type of treasure hunt using GPS. You can create a **cache** of toys or coins, and place them in an airtight container. You can also include a small notebook, called a log book, and a pencil. Then you hide it outside and figure out the exact GPS location.

Next you go onto the Internet to a geocaching Web site (with the help and approval of an adult) and submit your cache's location. You can look up other people's geocaches and go hunting for their treasure! When you find a cache, you get to take out a prize and replace it with something else so that there is plenty of treasure for future visitors. You write your name in the log book. Then you put the box right back where you found it.

A geocache can contain any items you like.

Enjoy the outdoors with your compass, some friends, and a treasure hunt you set up yourself.

Step #3: Challenge Your Friends and Family

Invite friends or family members to try your course. Give them the map and compass and see if they can find all the treasure. This is a good way for you and your friends to practice your orienteering skills!

There is a wide world out there. Are you curious about what it has in store for you? How will you find your way? If you have a compass, you have one of the tools you need to explore—and find all the treasures that await you.

Glossary

atoms (AT-uhms): The tiny building blocks that make up all things in the universe.

attract (uh-TRAKT): To pull closer.

axis (AK-sis): An imaginary line running from the North Pole to the South Pole of Earth around which Earth spins.

bearing (BAIR-ing): Where you want to go based on where you are, measured in degrees.

cache (kash): A collection of hidden items.

cardinal points (KAHR-dn-ul points): The main directions of north, south, east, and west.

core (kohr): The center of Earth.

declination (dek-luh-NAY-shuhn): The measure of the angle between true north (the North Pole) and magnetic north (the position a compass points to) measured in degrees.

horizon (huh-RAHY-zuhn): The line where it looks like the land or ocean meets the sky.

lichen (LAHY-kuhn): An organism that is a combination of fungus and algae that grows on trees and rocks.

lodestone (LOHD-stohn): A form of the mineral magnetite.

magnetic fields (mag-NET-ik feelds): The areas around magnets that pull objects close.

magnetic north (mag-NET-ik NORTH): The northern pole of the magnet-like force acting inside Earth.

navigate (nav-i-GAYT): To get from one place to another safely and without getting lost.

orienteering (or-ee-en-TEER-ing): Making one's way across terrain with the help of a map and compass.

orienteers (awr-ee-en-TEERS): Athletes that compete at orienteering.

pivoting (PIV-uh-ting): Spinning on one point.

poles (pohls): The ends of a magnet where the pull is the strongest.

resist (ri-ZIST): To push away.

satellites (SAT-ul-ahyts): Human-made objects placed into orbit around Earth that take in signals from Earth and send signals back down to the ground.

topographical maps (tuh-POG-ruh-fi-kuhl MAPS): A map with contour lines that show when the land gets higher or lower.

For More Information

Books

Atkins, Jeannine. *How High Can We Climb? The Story of Women Explorers.* New York: Farrar, Straus and Giroux, 2005.

Brunelle, Lynn. *Camp Out! From the Backyard to the Backwoods: The Ultimate Kids' Guide.* New York: Workman, 2007.

Dickinson, Rachel. *Tools of Navigation: A Kid's Guide to the History and Science of Finding Your Way.* White River Junction, VT: Nomad, 2005.

Kimmel, Elizabeth Cody. *The Look-It-Up Book of Explorers.* New York: Random House, 2004.

Stefoff, Rebecca. *World Historical Atlases: Exploration.* New York: Benchmark, 2005.

Young, Karen Romano. *Across the Wide Ocean: The Why, How, and Where of Navigation for Humans and Animals at Sea.* New York: Greenwillow, 2007.

Web Sites

BBC: A History of Navigation (www.bbc.co.uk/history/british/empire_seapower/launch_ani_navigation.shtml). Find an animated history of navigation at this site to see how navigation tools helped people explore the globe.

Boat Safe Kids: History of Navigation (www.boatsafe.com/kids/navigation.htm). Learn about early navigation and what tools sailors used to know the way to go.

Digital Topographical Maps (www.digital-topo-maps.com). You can zoom in and out of maps of the world and find topographical maps to print out when you want to explore an area with your compass.

Geocaching (www.geocaching.com). Become a part of the geocaching community on this Web site and discover the locations of almost a million geocaches worldwide.

Orienteering (www.4orienteering.com). Look up orienteering history, types, and information at this helpful site.

Scout Orienteering (www.scoutorienteering.com). If you are a scout, you can find the latest news about earning scouting orienteering badges here.

U.S. Orienteering Federation (www.us.orienteering.org). Visit this site to look up orienteering news, information about clubs and events in your area, and full descriptions of the basics of orienteering.

About the Author

Dana Meachen Rau is the author of more than 250 books for children from pre-school to middle school. She spends her days researching, writing, and trying out her projects in her sunny home office in Burlington, Connecticut.